# Paleo Slow Cooker Cookbook

# Paleo Slow Cooker Cookbook

Easy and Delicious Paleo Recipes

*Julia Grady*

Copyright © 2017 by Dylanna Publishing, Inc.
All rights reserved. This book or any portion thereof
may not be reproduced or used in any manner whatsoever without the express written permission of the publisher except for the use of
brief quotations in a book review.

First edition: 2017

Disclaimer/Limit of Liability

This book is for informational purposes only. The views expressed are those of the author alone, and should not be taken as expert, legal, or medical advice. The reader is responsible for his or her own actions.

Every attempt has been made to verify the accuracy of the information in this publication. However, neither the author nor the publisher assumes any responsibility for errors, omissions, or contrary interpretation of the material contained herein.

This book is not intended to provide medical advice. Please see your health care professional before embarking on any new diet or exercise program. The reader should regularly consult a physician in matters relating to his/her health and particularly with respect to any symptoms that may require diagnosis or medical attention.

# Contents

**INTRODUCTION** ............................................................................ **11**
**ABOUT THE PALEO DIET** ........................................................... **12**
**HEALTH BENEFITS OF THE PALEO DIET** ................................. **13**
**STOCKING YOUR PALEO KITCHEN** ........................................... **15**
**CLEANING OUT** ........................................................................... **15**
**RESTOCKING** .............................................................................. **15**
**SLOW COOKER ESSENTIALS** ................................................... **18**
**CHOOSING A SLOW COOKER** .................................................. **18**
**MINIMUM INTERNAL TEMPERATURE FOR DONENESS** ......... **19**
**CHICKEN AND POULTRY** .......................................................... **21**

    PALEO CHICKEN SOUP ........................................................ 22
    CHICKEN TIKKA MASALA..................................................... 24
    CHICKEN MOLE ..................................................................... 25
    CILANTRO LIME CHICKEN .................................................... 26
    SLOW-COOKED ROAST DUCK ............................................. 27
    CHICKEN CURRY ................................................................... 28
    GINGER-ORANGE CHICKEN ................................................ 30
    MEDITERRANEAN SAVORY CHICKEN STEW ..................... 31
    TERIYAKI WINGS ................................................................... 32
    HEARTY TURKEY STEW WITH ROOT VEGETABLES AND APPLES ....... 34
    CHICKEN FAJITA SOUP ........................................................ 36
    SLOW COOKER WHOLE CHICKEN ..................................... 37
    MOROCCAN CHICKEN TAGINE ........................................... 38
    CHICKEN AND SHRIMP GUMBO ......................................... 40
    KIMCHI CHICKEN .................................................................. 41
    CHICKEN CACCIATORE ....................................................... 42
    CHICKEN GUMBO ................................................................. 44

**BEEF AND VEAL** ........................................................................ **47**

| | |
|---|---|
| POT ROAST WITH ROOT VEGETABLES | 48 |
| BEEF STEW WITH BUTTERNUT SQUASH | 49 |
| PALEO BEEF CHILI | 50 |
| PALEO ITALIAN MEATBALLS | 52 |
| SLOW COOKER BOLOGNESE SAUCE | 54 |
| MEATBALL SOUP | 56 |
| STUFFED CABBAGE ROLLS | 59 |
| VEAL OSSO BUSCO | 60 |
| MOROCCAN BEEF TAGINE | 62 |
| PEPPERS STUFFED WITH SPINACH AND GROUND BEEF | 65 |
| SLOW COOKER SHORT RIBS | 66 |
| HUNGARIAN BEEF GOULASH | 69 |
| GROUND BEEF SWEET POTATO CASSEROLE | 70 |
| SLOW COOKER BEEF STEW AL LA CATHERINE | 71 |
| SLOW COOKER BEEF RAGU WITH ZOODLES | 72 |
| BEEF BOURGUIGNON | 74 |
| OXTAIL SOUP | 77 |

## LAMB ............................................................................... 79

| | |
|---|---|
| IRISH STEW | 80 |
| CURRY BRAISED LAMB LEG | 82 |
| SLOW COOKER LAMB WITH OLIVES AND APRICOTS | 83 |
| LAMB SHANKS AND CREMINI MUSHROOMS | 84 |
| SPICY INDIAN LAMB CURRY | 85 |

## PORK AND SAUSAGE .............................................................. 87

| | |
|---|---|
| KALE AND SAUSAGE SOUP | 88 |
| PORK SPARERIBS WITH HOMEMADE BARBECUE SAUCE | 90 |
| HERBED PORK ROAST | 91 |
| PULLED PORK WITH BARBECUE SAUCE | 92 |
| PEPPER PORK CHOPS WITH DRIED APRICOTS | 94 |
| PORK CHILI VERDE | 95 |
| SLOW-COOKED PORK CARNITAS | 96 |
| KALUA PORK | 97 |

## VEGETABLE DISHES ............................................................... 99

| | |
|---|---|
| SWEET POTATO COCONUT CURRY | 100 |

| VEGETARIAN VEGETABLE STEW | 102 |
| EGGPLANT RAGOUT/RATATOUILLE | 104 |
| INDIAN VEGETABLE CURRY | 106 |

## SEAFOOD ........................................................................................... 109

| SEAFOOD STEW | 110 |
| FISH CHOWDER | 111 |
| THAI SPICY SOUP WITH SHRIMP, TOM YUM KUNG | 112 |

## DESSERTS .......................................................................................... 115

| SLOW COOKER BAKED APPLES | 116 |
| PEAR CRUMBLE | 117 |
| PUMPKIN BREAD | 118 |
| BERRY COBBLER | 119 |
| SLOW COOKER APPLESAUCE | 120 |
| More Bestselling Titles from Dylanna Press | 123 |

# Introduction

WHETHER YOU'RE just starting out on the Paleo diet or have been eating Paleo for years, the *Paleo Slow Cooker Cookbook* is going to help you make delicious, healthy meals without spending a lot of time in the kitchen.

This book features the best Paleo slow cooker recipes, including dishes for all tastes and moods. Each of these recipes can be prepared in advance and then cooked in your slow cooker while you're off doing other things. There's really nothing better than coming home at the end of a hectic day to the smell of tonight's dinner already prepared and waiting to be eaten.

The slow cooker dishes in this collection feature fresh, whole foods that are cooked to be in line with the tenets of the Paleo diet—without refined sugars, grains, processed foods, or unhealthy oils. Included are a wide variety of recipes to appeal to every taste, classic dishes as well as new twists that just may become your new favorites.

In addition to the recipes, the book includes a brief overview of the Paleo diet—what it is, the health benefits of eating the Paleo way, how to stock your Paleo kitchen—as well as tips on how to get the most out of your slow cooker.

Thanks for reading and happy cooking!

# About the Paleo Diet

THE PALEO, or Paleolithic, diet is a way of eating that attempts to mimic as much as possible the diet and eating habits of humans during the pre-agricultural, or Paleolithic era. It is also known as the Stone Age diet, the hunter-gatherer diet, and the caveman diet. The focus of the diet is eating foods as close to their natural states as possible. The mainstays are organic, grass-fed meat, poultry, wild game, seafood, and fresh vegetables and fruits.

The theory behind the diet is simple. It reasons that humans evolved over the course of 2.5 million years, during a time when there was no agriculture and thus no grains, dairy products, legumes, processed foods, or refined sugars. Therefore, the human digestive system and nutritional needs are best adapted to the diet and foods that were eaten by our ancestors for hundreds of thousands of years. Modern humans have not yet adapted fully to the types of foods that have become available since the agricultural revolution which took place approximately 10,000 years ago. This maladaptation has led to many of the health problems we see today including diabetes, heart disease, obesity, and autoimmune disorders such as celiac disease and IBS.

Eating the Paleo way is not so much a diet as a lifestyle choice. If you want the long-term health benefits that the Paleo diet provides, then you need to be prepared to commit to it long term. Yes, the occasional non-Paleo treat is okay, but for the most part, this is a style of eating that requires commitment.

# Health Benefits of the Paleo Diet

THERE ARE many benefits to following the Paleolithic way of eating. Once you cut out processed foods, grains, and refined sugars, most people find they have never felt healthier. In addition to increased energy levels, the Paleo diet can help with weight loss, improve cholesterol levels, reduce triglycerides in the blood, stabilize blood sugar, and reduce inflammation throughout the body.

Why so many health benefits from the Paleo diet? Perhaps it is because the focus is on eating real food, without a lot of additives. By cutting out grains, dairy, sugar, and processed foods and adding in more fruits and vegetables, you will be dramatically increasing your intake of vitamins, minerals, and antioxidants.

Another reason the Paleo diet is good for your health is its focus on healthy fats. Specifically, omega-3 fatty acids, or polyunsaturated fatty acids (PUFAs). In a typical American diet the ratio of omega-6 fatty acids to omega-3 fatty acids can be as high as 15 to 1. This is in stark contrast to the recommended 1 to 1 ratio. This imbalance is due to our reliance on processed foods that are filled with refined vegetable oils, such as soybean oil, which are composed of omega-6 fatty acids. This imbalance can lead to chronic, systemic inflammation and is implicated in a host of diseases included asthma, cancer, heart disease, autoimmune disease, and obesity. By following the Paleo diet, you will balance this ratio and reverse the detrimental effects of the disproportionate level of omega-6s.

Another area where you will feel the benefits of the Paleo diet is in your gut health. By cutting out sugar, processed foods, and unhealthy fats, you will eliminate the main sources of stress and inflammation within your digestive tract. The natural bacteria that live in your intestinal system will thrive and you will have better overall gut health. Symptoms such as gas, bloating, constipation, diarrhea, and cramping will all be greatly relieved by following the Paleo way of eating.

Overall, when compared to the standard American diet (SAD), the Paleo diet is richer in nutrients and provides more of the micro- and macronutrients that the human body needs for optimum health. After following the Paleo diet, the majority of people report increased energy levels, better sleep quality, more stabilized moods, weight loss, better gut health, and a reduction in symptoms associated with inflammation including chronic pain, nasal congestion, and other allergic symptoms.

# Stocking Your Paleo Kitchen

A BIG PART of preparing meals without a lot of fuss is having the ingredients you need on hand. Keeping your pantry stocked with a few essentials will go a long way toward making it easy to prepare a quick and healthy Paleo meal.

## Cleaning Out

If you're committed to eating the Paleo way, the first thing you need to do is clean out your refrigerator, freezer, and pantry. Look carefully at all of the labels of everything in your kitchen. Get rid of anything that contains dairy, gluten, grains, legumes, sugar, and soy. Soy can be especially tricky to identify and is found in many types of products including the majority of processed foods.

## Restocking

Now that you've gotten rid of all the foods that may be causing problems, it's time to stock up on a few basics to keep on hand.

### Pantry Items

- Almond butter
- Almond flour
- Apple cider vinegar
- Apple sauce – no sugar added
- Arrowroot flour
- Avocado oil
- Baking soda
- Balsamic vinegar
- Broths – beef, chicken, vegetable, for times when you don't want to make homemade, buy organic, low-sodium
- Cacao powder/cacao nibs
- Coconut aminos – this is essential for making Asian-style and teriyaki dishes to use in place of soy sauce
- Coconut flour
- Coconut milk

- Coconut oil
- Dried fruits – apricots, cranberries, dates, goji berries, plums, raisins
- Dried mushrooms
- Fish sauce
- Ghee – make your own or purchase
- Herbs and spices– dried, grow your own fresh (allspice, black peppercorns, cardamom, cayenne pepper, cumin, ginger, oregano, thyme, garam masala, ground ancho chile, cinnamon, clove, red pepper flakes, paprika, curry powder, nutmeg, za'atar)
- Honey
- Lard
- Maple syrup
- Molasses
- Nut butters – almond, cashew, hazelnut, coconut
- Nut oils – almond, macadamia, walnut
- Nutritional yeast
- Nuts – raw cashews, almonds, macadamia, hazelnuts, pecans, pistachio, walnuts
- Olive oil
- Olives – green, black, Kalamata
- Pumpkin puree, canned (not pie filling)
- Rice vinegar
- Salmon, wild caught, canned
- Salsa
- Sardines
- Sea salt, Himalayan salt
- Tahini
- Tapioca starch
- Tomatoes – canned, paste, sauce
- Tuna, canned
- Vanilla extract
- White wine vinegar

# Freezer Items

- Bananas
- Berries
- Homemade soups and broth – freeze in single servings
- Meats
- Scallops
- Shrimp

# Refrigerator Items

- Bacon
- Eggs
- Fresh fruits and vegetables
- Garlic
- Lemons
- Limes
- Onions
- Salad greens

# Slow Cooker Essentials

Slow cookers are the greatest invention of all time. Okay, that might be a slight exaggeration, but there really is no better way to prepare delicious, flavorful meals with so little effort.

In addition, with a slow cooker, you can save money by buying cheaper cuts of meat because when cooked over 6-8 hours they will become tender and release their rich flavors.

## Choosing a Slow Cooker

There are many styles and sizes of slow cookers available today. They range in size from very small, which hold 1 1/2 to 2 quarts, to large, which hold up to 7 quarts. The most versatile and common size for a slow cooker is a 6-quart model and that is the size used for the recipes in this book. However, they can be adapted to a smaller or larger cooker size.

They come in variety of shapes as well—round, oval, even rectangular. An oval shape is recommended over a round one, because they tend to have less hot spots.

Some slow cooker models feature a stovetop safe insert, and if you are in the market for a new slow cooker then it is highly recommended that you choose this option. Many recipes require that you sauté or brown the meats and vegetables before adding them to the slow cooker and with these models there is no need to dirty another pan.

Another feature to look for is programmability. While manual slow cookers are cheaper, the ability to automatically switch to warm after a certain period of time can be a big plus if you work long days and don't want to come home and find an overcooked meal waiting for you.

## Tips for Using Your Slow Cooker

**Do not overfill your slow cooker.** Only fill about two-thirds full.

**Do not add frozen ingredients directly to slow cooker.** This can cause food to spend too much time in the food safety "danger zone" and potentially increase the chances of food-borne illnesses. Always thaw ingredients before adding to slow cooker.

**Cook meat and poultry to the FDA minimum internal temperature recommendations** (*see* table). Use an instant-read thermometer to test doneness.

**Do not lift cover while cooking more than absolutely necessary.** Doing so will cause the temperature to drop to potentially unsafe levels.

**Never reheat foods using the slow cooker.**

**Brown meats before adding to slow cooker.** Although it is nice to just throw all the ingredients in the slow cooker and let it cook, the majority of recipes will be enhanced by first browning the meats on the stovetop. Taking this extra step will lead to more flavorful dishes.

**Sautéing onions and garlic in oil for a couple of minutes before adding them to the slow cooker** will likewise increase the richness and flavor of the dish.

**Choose the right cut of meat.** Many people believe that the leanest cuts of meat are the best. However, when cooking in the slow cooker the opposite is true. When lean meats are cooked for a long time they can end up dry and tough. This is why slow cookers are ideal for more inexpensive, tougher, and fattier cuts of meat. The slow cooking breaks them down and leaves a tender, juicy piece of meat.

**Don't add too much liquid.** Since you are cooking with the lid on, very little liquid will evaporate during cooking. If too much liquid is added, you will have a thin, watery sauce.

## Minimum Internal Temperature for Doneness

The USDA recommends the following minimum internal temperatures for meats and poultry. To accurately measure temperature, stick and instant-read thermometer into the center of the meat, being careful to not let the thermometer touch the bone.

| Type of Meat | Minimum Internal Temperature (degrees F) |
|---|---|
| Beef | 145 |
| Pork | 145 |
| Lamb | 145 |
| Veal | 145 |
| Ground meat | 160 |
| Poultry | 165 |

# Chicken and Poultry

# PALEO CHICKEN SOUP

*This chicken soup is wonderful for helping to fight cold and flu.*

Servings: 4

1 tablespoon coconut oil or ghee

2 garlic cloves, minced

1 medium onion, chopped

6 stalks celery, chopped

4 carrots, chopped

2 pounds chicken pieces, skin removed

2 quarts water or chicken broth

2 teaspoons thyme

1 teaspoon oregano

1 teaspoon rosemary

Sea salt and freshly ground black pepper, to taste

1. Turn slow cooker on high setting, Add coconut oil or ghee.
2. Add garlic and onion and let heat for 5-6 minutes.
3. Add in remaining ingredients.
4. Cook on high setting for 5-6 hours or low setting for 8-10 hours.
5. Remove chicken pieces from slow cooker. Remove meat from bones, shred and return to pot. Discard bones.
6. Stir, adjust seasoning to taste, and serve.

# CHICKEN TIKKA MASALA

*This dish smells great and tastes even better!*

Servings: 4-6

2 tablespoons ghee or coconut oil

4 garlic cloves, minced

1 small yellow onion, diced

2 pounds chicken thighs, skin removed

1 ½ cups coconut milk

1 ½ cups crushed tomatoes

1 tablespoon fresh ginger, grated

1 small yellow onion, diced

1 tablespoon garam masala

2 teaspoons cumin

1 ½ teaspoons coriander

1 teaspoon turmeric

Sea salt and freshly ground black pepper to taste

1. Turn slow cooker to high setting. Add ghee or coconut oil.
2. Add garlic and onions and let cook for 5-6 minutes.
3. Add all remaining ingredients to slow cooker. Cover and cook on low setting for 3-4 hours.
4. Adjust seasoning and serve over Cauli-Rice.

# CHICKEN MOLE

*This chicken dish has a rich chocolate sauce.*

Serves: 4

2 tablespoons ghee

4 cloves garlic, minced

1 medium yellow onion, diced

2 pounds chicken & pieces, skin removed

1 can whole tomatoes

1 chipotle pepper, minced

1 teaspoon cumin

3 tablespoons chili powder

1 ½ teaspoons cinnamon

3 tablespoons tahini or almond butter

2 tablespoons cocoa powder, unsweetened

Sea salt and freshly ground pepper, to taste

Fresh cilantro, chopped, for garnish

1. Turn slow cooker on high. Add ghee.
2. Add garlic and onion and cook for 5-6 minutes.
3. Add chicken and all remaining ingredients to slow cooker. Stir.
4. Cover, turn heat to low, and cook for 5-6 hours or until chicken is tender.
5. Adjust seasoning and serve topped with fresh cilantro.

# CILANTRO LIME CHICKEN

*Very easy and delicious Mexican-style chicken.*

Servings: 6

3 pounds boneless, skinless chicken breasts

1 16-ounce jar of salsa

Juice of 1 lime

1 4-ounce can green chilies

3 cloves garlic

1 ½ teaspoons cumin

1 teaspoon oregano

1 teaspoon chili powder

1 teaspoon cayenne pepper

¼ cup fresh cilantro, chopped

1. Add all ingredients except for chicken to slow cooker. Mix with spoon to combine.
2. Add chicken and stir to coat with sauce.
3. Cook on high for 4 hours or on low setting for 6 to 8 hours.
4. Shred chicken and serve over shredded cabbage.

# SLOW-COOKED ROAST DUCK

*A slow cooker is a great way to cook a duck. They key is to raise the duck up above the fat drippings. You can use a wire rack for this or place the duck on top of some vegetables.*

Servings: 4-6

1 duck

1 lemon, cut into quarters

2 tablespoons ghee

4 large carrots, peeled and sliced

2 apples, peeled, cored, and cubed

2 stalks celery diced

1 medium yellow onion, diced

1 small bunch fresh thyme

2-3 sprigs fresh rosemary

Sea salt and freshly ground pepper, to taste

1. Remove giblets from duck, discard or save for later use. Rinse the duck with water and pat dry with paper towel. Season with salt and pepper, inside and out. Place lemon quarters inside of duck.
2. Turn slow cooker to higher setting. Add ghee.
3. Add carrots, apple, celery and onion to bottom of slow cooker.
4. Place the duck into the slow cooker on top of the layer of fruit and vegetables. Using fork, prick skin of duck in several places around the bird.
5. Cover and cook on high for 3-4 hours or on low setting for 6-7 hours or until internal temperature of duck reaches 185 degrees Fahrenheit. If crispier skin is desired, duck can be finished in 425-degree oven for 15 minutes.
6. Remove duck and place on serving platter. Arrange apple and vegetables around duck. Save any duck fat on bottom of slow cooker for future use.

# CHICKEN CURRY

*This chicken recipe is spicy and delicious.*

Servings:6

2 pounds chicken parts, skinless, quartered

3/4 cup coconut milk

1 cup chicken broth

2 tablespoon tomato paste

3 garlic cloves, minced

1 tablespoon ground ginger

6 tablespoon curry powder

2 bell peppers, chopped

1 yellow onion, thinly sliced

salt and pepper, to taste

1 dash red pepper flakes

1. In a slow cooker, combine all ingredients, except for the chicken. Mix well to blend. Add the chicken; ensure that all pieces are totally submerged in the liquid.
2. Cover and cook on low setting for about 7 hours or on high setting for about 5 hours.

# GINGER-ORANGE CHICKEN

## Servings: 4

2 pounds whole chickens, cut into parts

1/2 inch ginger, peeled, diced

1 garlic clove, peeled and smashed

2 large oranges, one juiced and one peeled and sliced

1 tomato, quartered

1 chili pepper

1 teaspoon sea salt

1. In a slow cooker, place chicken and the rest of the ingredients; cover and cook on high for about 3 hours.
2. Afterwards, remove the chicken onto a chopping board; chili pepper can also be removed if desired. Using an immersion blender, puree everything left in the pot.
3. Slice chicken into desired cuts, plate, glaze with sauce and serve.

# MEDITERRANEAN SAVORY CHICKEN STEW

Servings: 6

2 pounds chicken breasts, boneless, skinless, halved

2 tablespoon ghee

1 large yellow onion, diced

4 cloves garlic, chopped

1 teaspoon salt

1 28-oz. can crushed tomatoes

1/4 cup dried currants

1 bay leaf

1 teaspoon cumin

1/2 teaspoon ground coriander

1/4 teaspoon cinnamon

Pinch of red pepper flakes

1/4 cup honey

3 tablespoon fresh parsley, chopped

1. Turn slow cooker to high setting. Add ghee and let melt.
2. Add onion and garlic and cook for 5-6 minutes.
3. Add in all remaining ingredients except for parsley.
4. Turn heat to low and cook for 3-4 hours or until chicken is cooked through and tender.
5. Serve topped with fresh parsley.

# TERIYAKI WINGS

*These chicken wings have a thick and tasty sauce.*

Servings: 6-8

1/2 cup coconut aminos

1/4 cup honey

1/2 cup orange juice

½ pineapple juice

4 tablespoons rice vinegar

2 teaspoon arrowroot flour

2 tablespoon fresh ginger, grated

4 cloves garlic, minced

2 tablespoon sesame oil

2 teaspoon red pepper flakes

4 pounds chicken wings

1. Turn slow cooker to high.
2. In a large bowl, mix all ingredients except for chicken.
3. Place chicken in slow cooker. Pour marinade over chicken. Mix until chicken is thoroughly coated.
4. Cover and cook on high setting for 4 to 5 hours or low setting for 7-8 hours or until chicken is cooked through.

*Optional:* For a thicker sauce, remove wings from slow cooker and finish under broiler for 3-4 minutes.

# HEARTY TURKEY STEW WITH ROOT VEGETABLES AND APPLES

*This stew has an aromatic, flavorful sauce.*

Servings: 8

3 large sweet potatoes, peeled and cubed

4 apples, peeled, cored and cubed

2 large carrots, peeled and sliced

Sea salt and black pepper, taste.

4 boneless, skinless turkey thighs (about 3 ½ pounds)

1 teaspoon sage

1 teaspoon thyme

½ teaspoon ginger

1 red onion, diced

4 stalks celery, diced

3 cloves garlic, minced

1 cup apple juice

1 cup chicken stock

1. Turn slow cooker to high.
2. Spread sweet potatoes, apples, and carrots in bottom of cooker. Season with salt and pepper.
3. Place turkey thighs on top of sweet potato mixture. Season with sage, thyme, and ginger.
4. Top turkey with red onion, celery, and garlic. Pour in apple juice and chicken stock.
5. Cover and cook on low setting for 6-8 hours until vegetables and turkey are tender.

# CHICKEN FAJITA SOUP

*This soup is rich and flavorful and loaded with healthy veggies.*

Servings: 6

- 4 cloves garlic, minced
- 1 medium yellow onion, diced
- 1 bell pepper (red or green), diced
- 1 poblano pepper, diced
- 3 boneless, skinless chicken breasts (about 1 ½ pounds), cut into 2-inch pieces
- 4 cups chicken stock
- 1 can diced tomatoes (20 ounces)
- 1 can tomato sauce (14.5 ounces)
- 1 can green chilies (4 ounces)
- 1 tablespoon chili powder
- 1 teaspoon cayenne pepper
- 1 teaspoon paprika
- 1 teaspoon oregano
- 1 bay leaf

## *For topping*

- Juice of 1-2 limes
- 1 avocado, cubed
- ¼ cup fresh cilantro, chopped

1. Turn slow cooker to low setting.
2. Add all ingredients to slow cooker, except for toppings.
3. Cook for 5-6 hours or until chicken is cooked through (internal temperature of 160 degrees F). Adjust seasonings as desired.
4. Before serving, remove bay leaf and add lime juice.
5. Serve topped with avocado and cilantro.

# SLOW COOKER WHOLE CHICKEN

*This chicken is so easy it just might replace your store-bought rotisserie chicken.*

Servings: 4-6

1 pound baby carrots

1 medium onion, chopped

1 whole chicken (3-4 pounds)

1 tablespoon olive oil

4 cloves garlic, minced

1 teaspoon rosemary

1 teaspoon thyme

Sea salt and freshly ground black pepper, to taste

1. Spread baby carrots and chopped onion on bottom of slow cooker.
2. Rinse chicken under cold water and pat dry with paper towels. Brush skin with olive oil and place minced garlic inside chicken. Season chicken with rosemary, thyme, salt, and pepper. Place chicken in slow cooker.
3. Turn slow cooker to low setting and cook for 8 to 10 hours or until chicken is cooked through and juices run clear (internal temperature reaches 160 degrees F).

# MOROCCAN CHICKEN TAGINE

*An interesting blend of sweetness and spiciness that your taste buds are sure to love.*

Servings: 6

2 tablespoons olive oil

6 boneless, skinless chicken breasts (could substitute thighs), cut into bite-size pieces

1 eggplant, cubed

1 large yellow onion, sliced thin

4 large carrots, sliced thin

½ cup dried apricots, chopped

½ cup dried cranberries, chopped

2 1/2 cups chicken broth

3 tablespoons tomato paste

Juice of ½ lemon

3 garlic cloves, minced

2 teaspoons cumin

1 teaspoon cinnamon

1 tablespoon freshly grated ginger

1 teaspoon freshly ground black pepper

1. Place eggplant cubes in colander. Sprinkle liberally with salt. Let sit for 10-15 minutes. Rinse under cold running water. Pat dry with paper towels.
2. In a large skillet, heat olive oil over medium high heat. Add chicken and eggplant and cook until chicken is browned on all sides. Remove from heat.
3. Place chicken and eggplant into bottom of slow cooker. Add carrots, apricots, and cranberries.
4. In a large bowl, whisk together chicken broth, tomato paste, lemon juice, and spices. Pour over chicken and vegetables.
5. Cook on low setting for 7-8 hours or high setting for 4-5 hours or until chicken is cooked through and vegetables are tender.

# CHICKEN AND SHRIMP GUMBO

*This Cajun-inspired dish is easy and very flavorful.*

Servings: 6

2 pounds skinless, boneless chicken breasts or thighs, cut into bite-size pieces

2 cans stewed tomatoes (14.5 ounces each)

2 cups chicken broth

1 large yellow onion, chopped

1 bell pepper, chopped

3 stalks celery, chopped

4 cloves garlic, minced

1 teaspoon paprika

1 teaspoon ground red pepper

½ teaspoon garlic powder

½ teaspoon onion powder

½ teaspoon cayenne pepper

1 teaspoon freshly ground black pepper

1 pound medium shrimp, unthawed

1. Add all ingredients except shrimp to slow cooker. Stir gently to combine.
2. Cover and cook on low setting for 6 hours
3. Add shrimp and cook for another 15 minutes or until shrimp is opaque.

# KIMCHI CHICKEN

*Serve over Cauli-rice.*

Servings: 6

2 tablespoons ghee

4 scallions, sliced

4 garlic cloves, minced

1 tablespoon coconut aminos

1 tablespoon fresh ginger, grated

1 ½ cups chicken broth

2 pounds boneless, skinless chicken (breasts or thighs)

2 cups cabbage kimchi, drained

1. Turn slow cooker to high, add ghee. Add scallions and garlic and cook for 5-6 minutes.
2. Add coconut aminos, ginger, broth, and chicken, Stir gently to combine, making sure chicken is completed covered in sauce.
3. Cover, turn slow cooker down to low and cook for 4-5 hours.
4. Add kimchi to cooker, turn heat to high and cook for 30 minutes more.
5. Serve over Cauli-rice.

# CHICKEN CACCIATORE
*Easy to make and full of flavor*

Servings: 6

1 tablespoon olive oil

1 onion, diced

3 cloves garlic, minced

1 ½ pounds chicken thighs

1 (14 ounce) can diced tomatoes

2 cups chicken broth

2/3 cup sliced mushrooms

1 tablespoon oregano

½ teaspoon thyme

Salt and pepper, to taste

1. Pour olive oil into slow cooker. Add onion, garlic, chicken, tomatoes, broth, mushrooms, oregano, and thyme. Stir.
2. Cover and cook on low for 6-8 hours. Season with salt and pepper.

# CHICKEN GUMBO

*A healthy and flavorful gumbo.*

Servings: 6

2 pounds skinless, boneless chicken thighs, cubed

2 (14.5 ounce) cans stewed tomatoes

1 pound turkey sausage, casings removed and crumbled

2 cups chicken broth

1 large onion, chopped

1 green bell pepper, chopped

2 stalks celery, chopped

3 cloves garlic, minced

1 tablespoon Cajun seasoning

1/4 teaspoon cayenne pepper

1/4 teaspoon ground black pepper

1. Place all ingredients in slow cooker. Stir to combine.
2. Cover and cook on low 5-6 hours.

# Beef and Veal

# POT ROAST WITH ROOT VEGETABLES

*Slow cooking makes for a tender roast.*

Servings: 6

1 medium yellow onion, chopped

4 large carrots, sliced thin

1 rutabaga, peeled and chopped

1 turnip, peeled and chopped

1 (3 pound) chuck roast

Sea salt and freshly ground black pepper, to taste

1 can (15 ounce) tomato sauce

¼ maple syrup

3 cloves garlic, minced

3 teaspoons chili powder

1 teaspoon cumin

1. Place onion, carrot, rutabaga, and turnip in bottom of slow cooker.
2. Season roast with salt and pepper and place on top of vegetables.
3. In a bowl, mix together tomato sauce, maple syrup, garlic, and spices. Pour over beef.
4. Cover and cook on high setting for 8 hours or low setting for 11-12 hours.
5.

# BEEF STEW WITH BUTTERNUT SQUASH

*This aromatic stew with just a hint of sweetness is perfect for a crisp autumn day.*

Servings: 4

3 tablespoons olive oil

1 medium yellow onion, diced

3 cloves garlic, minced

2 pounds stew beef, cut into cubes

1 can (16 ounces) diced tomatoes

1 large butternut squash, trimmed and cut into bite-size cubes

4 cups beef broth

1 tablespoon rosemary

1 tablespoon thyme

Salt and freshly ground black pepper, to taste

1. Heat olive oil in large pot over medium heat. Add onions and garlic and sauté for 2-3 minutes. Add the beef cubes and cook until the beef is browned, about 5 minutes.
2. Transfer to slow cooker. Add the diced tomatoes, butternut squash, beef broth, rosemary, and thyme. Set cooker to low setting and cook for 8 hours. Add salt and freshly ground black pepper to taste.

# PALEO BEEF CHILI

*This beanless chili has a rich smoky flavor. Slow cooking lets the flavors meld together.*

Servings: 6

1 tablespoon coconut oil

1 large yellow onion, chopped

1 large green bell pepper, chopped

1 large red bell pepper, chopped

6 garlic cloves, minced

1 1/2 pounds ground beef

1 pound ground pork

2 tablespoons chili powder

1 tablespoon cumin

2 teaspoons dried oregano

2 teaspoons cayenne pepper

1 teaspoon cocoa powder, unsweetened

2 teaspoons Worcestershire sauce

1 can (28 ounces) crushed tomatoes

2 tablespoons tomato paste

Salt and freshly ground black pepper, to taste

1. Heat coconut oil in large pot over medium heat. Add onions, bell peppers, and garlic and sauté until vegetables are tender, about 7-9 minutes.
2. Add ground beef and pork to pot and continue cooking and stirring until meat is browned, 3-4 minutes.
3. Transfer to slow cooker. Add spices and all remaining ingredients to slow cooker. Stir to mix. Cover and cook on low setting for 8 hours or high setting for 6 hours.

# PALEO ITALIAN MEATBALLS

*Serve these meatballs over zucchini noodles (Zoodles) for a satisfying dinner.*

Servings: 4-6

- 1 ½ pounds ground beef
- ½ pound ground pork
- 1/2 cup almond meal
- ¼ cup fresh parsley, chopped
- 3 garlic cloves, minced
- 1 small yellow onion, finely chopped
- 1 egg, beaten
- 3 cups marinara sauce
- 1 16-ounce can crushed tomatoes
- 1 14-ounce can tomato puree
- 1 teaspoon oregano
- 1 teaspoon marjoram
- 1 teaspoon black pepper

1. In a large bowl, mix together beef, almond meal, parsley, garlic, onion, and egg. Shape into balls about 2 inches in diameter.
2. In a slow cooker mix together marinara sauce, crushed tomatoes, tomato puree, oregano, marjoram, and pepper. Add meatballs to sauce.
3. Cover and cook on low setting for 6 to 8 hours.
4. Serve over zucchini noodles.

# SLOW COOKER BOLOGNESE SAUCE

*This sauce has a distinct, rich, meaty flavor.*

Servings: 8

4 slices bacon, cut into small pieces

1 tablespoon olive oil

1 medium yellow onion, diced

1 carrot, chopped fine

2 celery stalks, chopped fine

1 pound ground beef (preferably grass-fed)

½ cup tomato paste

½ cup almond milk

1 ½ cups beef stock

½ cup red wine (alcohol will evaporate during cooking)

Sea salt and freshly ground black pepper, to taste

1. Sauté bacon in large frying pan for 5 minutes over medium heat. Add olive oil, onion, carrots, and celery and cook for another 5-6 minutes. Add ground beef to pan and cook until browned, stirring occasionally, about 4-5 minutes.
2. Add tomato paste, almond milk, beef stock, and red wine to slow cooker. Stir well to dissolve tomato paste. Add meat mixture to slow cooker. Season with salt and pepper.
3. Cover and cook on low for 6 hours.

# MEATBALL SOUP

*This hearty soup is perfect on a cold winter day.*

Servings: 6

## For the meatballs:

- 1 pound ground beef
- ½ pound ground pork
- 1/4 cup almond meal
- 3 garlic cloves, minced
- 1 small yellow onion, finely chopped
- 1 egg, beaten
- 1 tablespoon Italian seasoning
- 1 teaspoon black pepper
- ½ teaspoon sea salt
- 2 tablespoons olive oil

## For the soup:

- 4 slices bacon, cut into pieces
- 3 cloves garlic, minced
- 1 medium zucchini, chopped
- 1 medium yellow squash, chopped
- 2 carrots, sliced thin
- 1 small onion, diced fine
- 1 teaspoon oregano
- 1 teaspoon marjoram
- 1 teaspoon garlic powder
- 4 cups chicken broth
- 1 can (14 ounces) diced tomatoes

1. In a large bowl, mix together all ingredients for meatballs except for olive oil. Form into balls about 1 ½ to 2 inches in diameter.
2. Heat olive oil in large skillet over medium heat. Add meatballs and cook until all sides are browned. Remove meatballs and set aside. Add bacon to pan and sauté for 4-5 minutes. Add garlic and sauté for another 2 minutes.
3. Place bacon and garlic (along with drippings) into slow cooker. Place meatballs on top.
4. Add in all remaining ingredients. Stir gently to mix.
5. Cover and cook on low setting for 8 hours or on high setting for 5 hours.

# STUFFED CABBAGE ROLLS

*Delicious!*

Servings: 6

12 large cabbage leaves

½ cauliflower

1 large carrot, sliced

1 pound ground beef

½ pound ground pork

1 egg

¼ cup beef stock

1 tablespoon lemon juice

Sea salt and freshly ground black pepper, to taste

2 cups tomato sauce

1. Place cabbage leaves in pot of boiling salted water for 1-2 minutes until leaves soften. Rinse under cold water and set aside.
2. Cut cauliflower into large florets and place in food processor along with the carrot. Process until it reaches the consistency of rice.
3. In a large bowl, combine cauliflower-carrot mixture, beef, pork, egg, stock, and lemon juice. Season with salt and pepper.
4. Place cabbage leaves on flat surface. Place 1/12 of filling mixture near bottom of leaves. Roll once, tuck each end in, then continue to roll.
5. Place cabbage leaves in crock pot. Add tomato sauce on top.
6. Cover and cook on low setting for 8-9 hours or high setting for 5-6 hours.

*Tip:* To making rolling cabbage leaves easier, slice off the spine of the cabbage to make it level with rest of leaf.

# VEAL OSSO BUSCO

*This classic Italian veal dish features a flavorful sauce.*

Servings: 6

1 sprig rosemary

1 sprig thyme

1 bay leaf

2 whole cloves

Cheesecloth

Twine

3 veal shanks (1 pound each)

Sea salt and freshly ground pepper, to taste

Almond flour, for dredging

½ cup olive oil

1 small onion, diced

1 carrot, diced

1 celery stalk, diced

1 tablespoon tomato paste

1 cup white wine

3 cups chicken stock

3 tablespoons fresh flat leaf parsley, chopped

1 tablespoon lemon zest

1. Cut piece of cheesecloth to make bouquet garni. Place in rosemary, thyme, bay leaf, and cloves. Secure with twine.
2. Season veal shanks with salt and pepper. Dredge in almond flour, shake off excess.
3. Heat olive oil in large pot. Add veal shanks and brown on all sides, about 2-3 minutes per side.
4. Add tomato paste, wine, and stock to bottom of slow cooker, stir mixture well to dissolve tomato paste. Add onion, carrot, celery, bouquet garni, and veal shanks to slow cooker. Mix gently to cover veal shanks with sauce.
5. Cover and cook on low heat for 6-8 hours until veal is very tender and falling off bone.
6. Serve topped with parsley and lemon zest.

# MOROCCAN BEEF TAGINE

*Cooking this dish in the slow cooker allows the flavors to deepen and develop.*

Servings: 4 to 6

## Spice rub

- 1 tablespoon cumin
- 1 tablespoon cinnamon
- 1 tablespoon ginger
- 1 tablespoon paprika
- 1 teaspoon nutmeg
- 1 teaspoon turmeric
- 1 teaspoon sea salt
- 1 teaspoon freshly ground black pepper

## For the stew

- 1 ½ pounds stew beef
- 2 tablespoon olive oil
- 1 medium onion, chopped
- 1 bunch fresh coriander
- 1 (14 ounce) can chopped tomatoes
- 3 cups vegetable or beef stock
- 1 small zucchini, chopped
- 1 large carrots, sliced thin
- 1 red bell pepper, sliced thin
- 3-4 prunes, chopped
- Sea salt and ground black pepper, to taste

1. In a small bowl, mix together all of the ingredients for the spice rub.
2. Place beef in large zip lock bag. Add spice mixture and shake to thoroughly coat meat. Put in refrigerator for a couple of hours or overnight.
3. Heat olive oil in large skillet over medium heat. Add beef and brown on all sides, about 5 minutes.
4. Add meat to slow cooker. Add all remaining ingredients. Stir to combine.
5. Cover and cook on high setting for 5-6 hours or low setting for 7-8 hours.

# PEPPERS STUFFED WITH SPINACH AND GROUND BEEF

*These scrumptious stuffed peppers have just a hint of cinnamon*

Servings: 6

1 medium yellow onion, diced

3 cloves garlic, minced

1 pound ground beef

2 cups baby spinach, chopped

2 eggs

1 1/2 tablespoons cinnamon

1 tablespoon cardamom

Salt and freshly ground black pepper, to taste

6 large bell peppers

1 cup tomato sauce

1. In a large bowl, combine onion garlic, ground beef, baby spinach, eggs, cinnamon, cardamom, salt, and pepper.
2. Cut tops of peppers and remove seeds. Fill each pepper with 1/6 of ground beef mixture.
3. Place peppers in bottom of slow cooker. Pour tomato sauce over peppers.
4. Cover and cook on high for 4 hours or low for 6 hours, until beef is cooked through.

# SLOW COOKER SHORT RIBS

*This recipe only takes 10 minutes of hands-on time.*

Servings: 4

1 tablespoon coconut oil

2 pounds beef short ribs, grass-fed

Salt and freshly ground black pepper, to taste

3 tablespoons balsamic vinegar

1 tablespoon Dijon mustard

1/2 cup water

1. Heat coconut oil in heavy skillet over medium-high heat until oil is hot. Add the ribs and sear on all sides. Season with salt and pepper.
2. Transfer ribs to slow cooker.
3. In a small bowl, whisk together vinegar, mustard, and water. Pour over ribs.
4. Set slow cooker to low and let cook for eight hours.
5. Serve with steamed veggies.

# HUNGARIAN BEEF GOULASH

*This version of beef goulash replaces the traditional sour cream with paleo sour cream.*

Servings: 6

2 pound steak, cut into 1-inch cubes

1 medium onion, sliced thin

1 carrot, diced

2 stalks celery, diced

2 hot red peppers, sliced

3 cloves garlic, minced

2 tablespoons coconut flour

2 teaspoons paprika

1 ½ teaspoons garlic salt

1 teaspoon freshly ground black pepper

1 (14 ounce) can diced tomatoes

1 bay leaf

1 cup Paleo sour cream (recipe below)

1. Place steak cubes, onions, carrot, peppers, and celery in bottom of slow cooker.
2. In a small bowl, combine garlic, coconut flour, paprika, garlic salt, and pepper. Pour over meat and mix to combine.
3. Add diced tomatoes and bay leaf.
4. Cover and cook on low for 8-10 hours or high for 6-7 hours until steak is tender.
5. Remove bay leaf and discard. Stir in sour cream mixture. Cook for another 15 minutes, until hot.
6. Serve over Zoodles.

## Paleo Sour Cream

- 1 cup coconut milk, full fat
- 2 tablespoons lemon juice
- ¼ teaspoon sea salt

1. Open can of coconut milk and drain out liquid milk, leaving cream.
2. Scoop cream in to a bowl, Whisk in lemon juice and salt. Adjust lemon juice and salt to taste.

# GROUND BEEF SWEET POTATO CASSEROLE

*This is a very hearty and filling dish*

Servings: 6-8

4 slices bacon, chopped up

1 large white onion, diced

1 large red pepper, diced

3 garlic cloves, minced

2 pounds of ground beef

1 tablespoon cayenne pepper

2 teaspoons paprika

2 teaspoons oregano

Freshly ground black pepper, to taste

6 eggs

Coconut oil, for greasing

3 large sweet potatoes, peeled and sliced thin

1. In a large skillet, heat bacon until crisp. Remove from pan and set aside, keeping bacon grease in pan.
2. Add onions, garlic, and peppers to pan and sauté for 2-3 minutes until they start to soften. Add ground beef and cook another couple of minutes until beef is browned. Add cayenne pepper, oregano, paprika, and black pepper, mix well.
3. In a bowl, beat eggs. Add pepper to taste.
4. Grease bottom of slow cooker with coconut oil. Line bottom of slow cooker with a layer of sweet potato slices.
5. Top with a layer of ground beef mixture (1/4 of mixture). Sprinkle with ¼ bacon.
6. Repeat layers until you run out of ingredients.
7. Pour eggs over top of layers.
8. Cook on low setting for 5-6 hours.

# SLOW COOKER BEEF STEW A LA CATHERINE

*This recipe is a family favorite.*

Servings: 6

1 1/2 pounds stewed beef meat, cubed

2 tablespoons ghee

1 large onion, cubed

1 1/2 cups baby carrots

1 1/2 cups squash or cauliflower, diced

3 bay leaves

10 oz. can tomato soup

1 cup water

1 tablespoon steak sauce

1 (1 oz.) package dry onion soup mix

Juice of ½ lemon

1/2 teaspoon sea salt

½ teaspoon black pepper

1. In a slow cooker, combine beef and ghee. Place on top the vegetables and bay leaves.
2. In a bowl, mix together tomato soup, water, steak sauce, lemon juice, and onion soup mix. Pour in over meat and vegetables. Season with salt and pepper.
3. Cook on low for 8-10 hours.

# SLOW COOKER BEEF RAGU WITH ZOODLES

*The prep time for this is quick, but let the meat slow-cook for hours for a rich, deep flavor.*

Servings: 4

- 2 tablespoons olive oil
- 1/2 yellow onion, finely chopped
- 2 celery sticks, chopped
- 2 medium carrots, peeled and chopped
- 1 1/2 pounds ground beef, preferably grass-fed
- 2 large cans whole peeled tomatoes
- 1 cup beef stock
- 1/2 cup water
- 1/3 cup balsamic vinegar
- 1 recipe Zoodles (see below)

1. Heat oil in large skillet over medium-high heat. Add onion and sauté for 1-2 minutes. Add celery and carrots and continue cooking for an additional 1-2 minutes. Add ground beef to pan and cook, stirring until beef is browned. Remove pan from heat.
2. Add ground beef mixture to slow cooker. Add peeled tomatoes, beef stock, water, and balsamic vinegar. Turn slow cooker to high, and let simmer for 3-4 hours.
3. Serve over Zoodles.

## Zoodles

Servings: 4

- 4 medium zucchini
- Salt and freshly ground pepper to taste

1. Using either your vegetable spiral slicer or julienne peeler, cut zucchini into long skinny noodles.
2. These can be cooked by stir frying in either olive oil or coconut oil for 2-3 minutes until tender or microwave in a covered, microwave-safe dish for about 1.5 to 2 minutes.

# BEEF BOURGUIGNON

*Rich and robust flavor.*

Servings: 8

¼ cup olive oil

2 pounds beef, cut into cubes

Sea salt, to taste

Freshly ground black pepper, to taste

2 large onions, sliced

4 large carrots, sliced

8 ounces fresh mushrooms, sliced

2 cloves garlic, minced

¼ teaspoon dried marjoram

½ teaspoon dried thyme

1 bay leaf

2 teaspoons tomato paste

1/2 cup dry red wine

1 cup beef broth


1. Heat oil in large skillet over medium heat. Add beef cubes, season with salt and pepper, and sear on all sides, about 2-3 minutes per side.
2. Transfer beef cubes to slow cooker.
3. In same skillet, sauté onions, carrots, mushrooms, and garlic for 5 minutes. Season with salt and pepper. Transfer vegetables to slow cooker.
4. Add, marjoram, thyme, bay leaf, tomato paste, wine, and beef broth to slow cooker. Stir to combine. Cover and cook on low for 8 hours.

# OXTAIL SOUP

*Tasty soup with the healing properties of bone broth.*

Servings: 6

2 tablespoons ghee

1 pound oxtail, cut into pieces

1 large onion, chopped

4 cups beef bone broth

3 large carrots, sliced

1 pound potatoes, peeled and cubed (optional - substitute sweet potatoes if preferred)

2 stalks celery, chopped

1 (14.5 ounce) can stewed tomatoes

Sea salt and freshly ground black pepper, to taste

1. Heat ghee in large skillet over medium heat. Add oxtail and onion and saute 5-6 minutes until onion is softened and oxtail is browned. Transfer to slow cooker.

2. Add bone broth, carrots, potatoes, celery, and stewed tomatoes to slow cooker. Season with salt and pepper and stir to combine.

3. Cover and cook on low for 8 hours.

*Lamb*

# IRISH STEW

*This is a hearty stew.*

Servings: 6-8

- 2 pounds lamb roast, cut into 1" pieces
- 1lb small red potatoes, cut into bite size pieces
- 1 medium onion, sliced
- 2 large carrots, sliced
- 1 large parsnip, sliced
- 3 stalks celery, chopped
- 3 cups chicken broth
- 2 teaspoon fresh thyme, chopped
- 1 teaspoon salt
- 1 teaspoon pepper

1. Combine all ingredients in slow cooker. Stir to combine.
2. Cover and cook on low for 8 hours.

# CURRY BRAISED LAMB LEG

*This spicy dish is very simple to prepare in a slow cooker.*

Servings: 8

4 pounds leg of lamb, trimmed

1 tablespoon coconut oil

1 whole onion, diced

3 cloves garlic, minced

1-inch piece ginger, minced

3 serrano pepper chilies, minced

2 (16-oz.) cans tomatoes

3 teaspoons fennel

2 teaspoon cumin

1 teaspoon cinnamon

1 teaspoon cardamom

1/2 teaspoon black pepper

½ teaspoon ground cloves

1/4 teaspoon coriander

1/2 teaspoon nutmeg

1/4 teaspoon safflower

1 teaspoon turmeric

1 tsp salt

1. In a large skillet, heat oil over medium high heat. Cook sides of lamb legs until browned. Set lamb aside. In the same pan, cook onions, garlic, pepper chilies, and ginger for about 5 minutes or until tender. Transfer to slow cooker.
2. Add in tomatoes to slow cooker. Add in all spices. Stir to combine. Add lamb and mix.
3. Cover and cook on low for about 10 hours.

# SLOW COOKER LAMB WITH OLIVES AND APRICOTS

Servings: 4

1 ½ pounds lamb, cut into bite size pieces

1 medium yellow onion, chopped

4 large carrots, sliced

3 cloves garlic, minced

½ cup dried apricots, chopped

½ cup green olives, pitted

2 tablespoons coconut flour

1 teaspoon paprika

1 teaspoon ground cumin

1 teaspoon cinnamon

½ teaspoon ginger

Sea salt and freshly ground black pepper, to taste

Lemon wedges, for serving

1. Combine all ingredients except for lemon wedges in slow cooker. Mix to combine.
2. Cover and cook on high for 4-5 hours or low for 7-8 hours until lamb and vegetables are tender.
3. Serve with lemon wedges.

# LAMB SHANKS AND CREMINI MUSHROOMS

Servings: 6

1 pound cremini mushrooms, washed, cut in halves

2 carrots, chopped

2 celery stalks, chopped

1 medium onion, chopped

4 cloves garlic, minced

1 red bell pepper, sliced

1 (14 ounce) can of crushed tomatoes

3 tablespoons tomato paste

1 teaspoon rosemary

½ teaspoon cinnamon

Sea salt and freshly ground black pepper, to taste

2 ½ pounds lamb shanks, trimmed of excess fat

1 cup beef broth

1. Place mushrooms, carrots, celery, onion, garlic, and red pepper into slow cooker.
2. Add crushed tomatoes, tomato paste, rosemary, cinnamon, salt, and pepper. Mix.
3. Add lamb shanks. Pour in broth.
4. Cover and cook on low for 8 hours until vegetables and lamb are tender.

# SPICY INDIAN LAMB CURRY

Servings: 6

2 tablespoon coconut oil

2 pound lamb stew meat, cubed

3 large carrots, sliced

1 large onion, diced

4 cloves garlic, minced

1 cup chicken broth

3 tablespoons curry powder

1 teaspoon ground ginger

1 teaspoon paprika

1 teaspoon ground cumin

1 teaspoon sea salt

1 ½ teaspoons freshly ground black pepper

1 cup coconut milk

1 (14.5 ounce) can stewed tomatoes

1. Heat coconut oil in large skillet over medium heat. Add lamb cubes and sear on all sides, 2-3 minutes per side. Transfer to slow cooker.
2. In same skillet, sauté carrots, onions, and garlic until softened, 4-5 minutes. Transfer to slow cooker.
3. Add chicken broth, curry powder, ginger, paprika, cumin, salt, pepper, coconut milk, and stewed tomatoes. Stir to combine.
4. Cover and cook on low for 6 to 8 hours or high for 4 to 5 hours.

# PORK AND SAUSAGE

# KALE AND SAUSAGE SOUP

*This full-flavored soup is very easy to make.*

Servings: 4

1 tablespoon ghee

1 pound Italian sausage, cut into small pieces

6 small red potatoes

1 medium yellow onion, chopped

2 cloves garlic, minced

1 (28 ounce) can diced tomatoes

2 tablespoons tomato paste

1 cup vegetable broth or water

Sea salt and freshly ground black pepper, to taste

1 bunch kale, stems trimmed, chopped

1/3 cup coconut milk

1. Add ghee, sausage, potatoes, onion, tomatoes, tomato paste, garlic, broth, salt, and pepper to slow cooker. Stir to combine. Add kale.
2. Cover and cook on high for 4 to 5 hours or on low for 7 to 8 hours.
3. Before serving, pour in coconut milk. Stir and heat on high for 10-15 minutes.

# PORK SPARERIBS WITH HOMEMADE BARBECUE SAUCE

*Spareribs cooked in the slow cooker is much easier than on the grill. These ribs are so tender the meat practically falls off the bone.*

Servings: 4

## For the Barbecue Sauce

- 6 medium tomatoes, chopped small
- 1 onion, chopped small
- 3 cloves garlic
- 1 teaspoon chili powder
- 1 teaspoon cayenne
- ½ teaspoon paprika
- ½ teaspoon coriander
- 1 bay leaf
- ½ teaspoon black pepper
- ½ teaspoon salt
- 1 teaspoon balsamic vinegar
- 2 tablespoons apple cider vinegar
- 1 tablespoon coconut aminos
- 2 tablespoons honey

## For the Ribs

- 3 pounds pork ribs

1. In a large pot, add all of the ingredients for the barbecue sauce. Stir well. Cover and cook over medium-high heat for about 20 minutes, stirring occasionally until tomatoes break down and sauce starts to thicken.
2. Remove from heat, remove bay leaf, and pour mixture into blender or food processor (a stick blender is good for this also). Process until sauce is smooth.
3. Place ribs into slow cooker. Pour sauce over ribs.
4. Cover and cook on low setting for 3 to 4 hours until ribs are tender.

# HERBED PORK ROAST

*If you like garlic, you will love this pork roast.*

Servings: 6

4 garlic cloves, chopped

3 ½-4 pound pork roast, boneless

1 teaspoon thyme

1 teaspoon sea salt

½ teaspoon sage

½ teaspoon ground cloves

1 teaspoon grated lemon rind

½ cup water

1. Cut small slits all over roast and insert pieces of garlic.
2. Sprinkle roast with thyme, salt, sage, cloves, and lemon rind.
3. Pour water into bottom of slow cooker. Add pork roast
4. Cover and cook on low for 8-9 hours until pork is tender.

# PULLED PORK WITH BARBECUE SAUCE

*This is recipe is so easy, yet the results are pretty amazing.*

Servings: 8

3-4 pound pork roast, boneless

## For the spice rub

3 tablespoons paprika

1 tablespoons sea salt

1 tablespoon black pepper

1 tablespoon garlic powder

1/2 tablespoon dry mustard

## For the barbecue sauce

6 medium tomatoes, chopped small

1 onion, chopped small

3 cloves garlic

1 teaspoon chili powder

1 teaspoon cayenne

½ teaspoon paprika

½ teaspoon coriander

1 bay leaf

½ teaspoon black pepper

½ teaspoon salt

1 teaspoon balsamic vinegar

2 tablespoons apple cider vinegar

1 tablespoon coconut aminos

2 tablespoons honey

1. In a small bowl, mix together all of the spice rub ingredients.
2. Cut the pork into medium size chunks. Put into slow cooker. Season meat with spice rub mixture. Mix gently to thoroughly coat pork.
3. Cover and cook on low setting for 10 hours or high setting for 6 hours, until meat is tender and easily pulls apart.
4. Remove pork from slow cooker and transfer to large serving platter. Using fork, pull pork into shreds. Serve with barbecue sauce.

## To make the barbecue sauce
1. In a large pot, add all of the ingredients for the barbecue sauce. Stir well. Cover and cook over medium-high heat for about 20 minutes, stirring occasionally until tomatoes break down and sauce starts to thicken.
2. Remove from heat, remove bay leaf, and pour mixture into blender or food processor (a stick blender is good for this also). Process until sauce is smooth.

# PEPPER PORK CHOPS WITH DRIED APRICOTS

*Marinating overnight gives these pork chops a zesty taste.*

Servings: 4

1 cup vegetable broth

3 tablespoons black peppercorns, crushed

2 tablespoons honey

1 teaspoon sea salt

4 pork chops, thick cut, bone-in

2 tablespoons olive oil

1 large onion, chopped

3 ounces dried apricots

1 1/2 cups chicken broth

1 tablespoon freshly ground black pepper

1 teaspoon thyme

1. Place vegetable broth, peppercorns, honey, sea salt, and pork chops into a large gallon-size zip lock bag. Shake gently to mix. Place in refrigerator for a couple of hours or preferably overnight.
2. Remove pork chops from bag. Discard liquid.
3. Heat olive oil in large skillet over medium-high heat. Add pork chops and sauté for a couple of minutes on each side to brown.
4. Place onion and apricots in slow cooker. Place pork chops on top. Pour in chicken broth and season with pepper and thyme.
5. Cover and cook on low for 6-7 hours or high for 4-5 hours until pork is tender.

# PORK CHILI VERDE

*Let the slow cooker do the work for this melt-in-your-mouth, spicy dish.*

Servings: 6

2 tablespoons olive oil

2 1/2 pound pork shoulder, cut into 1-inch cubes

1 pound tomatillos, husk removed, diced

1 can (6 ounces) Hatch green chilies

1 large yellow onion, diced

6 garlic cloves, minced

2 cups beef stock

1 tablespoon cumin

1 tablespoon oregano

1 tablespoon coriander

1/2 cup fresh cilantro, minced

Salt and freshly ground black pepper, to taste

1. Heat olive oil in a large skillet over medium-high heat. Add pork cubes and brown on all sides, about 4-5 minutes. Remove pork and set aside.
2. Lower heat to medium and add the tomatillos, chilies, onion, and garlic. Sauté for 4-5 minutes or until onions start to soften. Remove from heat and transfer to slow cooker.
3. Add pork, beef stock, cumin, oregano, coriander, cilantro, salt, and pepper to slow cooker. Cover and cook on low for 6-7 hours or until pork is tender.

# SLOW-COOKED PORK CARNITAS

*The slow-cooked pork is melt-in-your-mouth tender.*

Servings: 6

1 teaspoon cumin

1 teaspoon coriander

1 teaspoon salt

1 teaspoon freshly ground black pepper

1 teaspoon oregano

1 teaspoon garlic powder

1 teaspoon cinnamon

2 1/2-3 pound pork shoulder

1 tablespoon olive oil

1 medium Vivaldi onion, chopped

1 can green chiles

1 cup beef stock

1 bay leaf

1. In a bowl, combine first seven ingredients (through cinnamon). Rub this mixture all over pork shoulder coating all sides thoroughly.
2. Put on olive oil and onion into bottom of slow cooker. Place pork shoulder into slow cooker. Add green chilies, beef stock and bay leaf. Cover and cook on low for 8-10 hours until pork comes apart easily with fork. Alternatively, cook on high for 4 hours and then turn down to low for additional 2-3 hours. Add additional salt and pepper to taste. Shred pork into bite-sized pieces.
3. Serve on top of bed of romaine lettuce and top with any (or all) of the following: guacamole, salsa, chopped tomato, chopped red onion, shredded cheese (if you eat dairy).

# KALUA PORK

*Easy and delicious, sure to become a family favorite.*

Servings: 8-10

1/2 cup water

1/2 cup coconut aminos

1 (4 pound) pork butt roast

1 tablespoon liquid smoke

Sea salt

2 bunches scallions, chopped

3 cloves garlic, chopped

1. Pour water and coconut aminos into bottom of slow cooker. Add pork roast. Pierce roast with fork several times and pour liquid smoke onto roast. Sprinkle generously with sea salt. Cover with scallions and garlic.
2. Cover and cook on low for 8-9 hours.

# Vegetable Dishes

# SWEET POTATO COCONUT CURRY

*This is a mild curry that makes a delicious side to fish or chicken.*

Servings: 4

1 tablespoon coconut oil

1 small yellow onion, diced

3 clove garlic, minced

1 teaspoon cumin powder

½ teaspoon turmeric

½ teaspoon cardamom

½ teaspoon cinnamon

½ teaspoon ground ginger

1 can diced tomatoes

4 medium sweet potatoes, peeled and cut into bit-size cubes

1 can (15 ounces) coconut milk

Salt and freshly ground black pepper, to taste

Flat leaf parsley for garnish

1. Add all ingredients to slow cooker. Mix to combine.
2. Cover and cook on low setting for 4-5 hours until sweet potatoes are tender.
3. Serve hot, topped with fresh parsley for garnish.

# VEGETARIAN VEGETABLE STEW

*This is perfect as a side dish or a light meal.*

Servings: 6

4 large carrots, sliced

2 medium turnips, peeled and cubes

1 large onion, sliced thin

3 garlic cloves, minced

1 zucchini, sliced

2 yellow squash, sliced

2 cups vegetable broth

1/2 teaspoon red pepper flakes

1 teaspoon thyme

Sea salt and freshly ground black pepper, to taste

7. Combine all ingredients in slow cooker.
8. Cover, and cook on low for 5-6 hours or on high for 3-4 hours.

# EGGPLANT RAGOUT/RATATOUILLE

*This versatile recipe can be used as topping for Zoodles, as a side dish, or eaten as a stand-alone meal.*

Servings: 8

2 large onions, diced

1 large eggplant, cut into 2-inch pieces

4 yellow squash, sliced

3 cloves garlic, minced

1 large green pepper, deseeded, and chopped

2 large tomatoes, chopped

1 (6 ounce) can tomato paste

1 teaspoon basil

1 teaspoon oregano

1 teaspoon sea salt

1/2 teaspoon black pepper

2 tablespoons fresh parsley, chopped

3 tablespoons olive oil

1 teaspoon red pepper flakes (optional)

1. Layer 1/2 of vegetables to slow cooker in this order: onions, eggplant, squash, garlic, peppers, tomatoes.
2. Sprinkle with half of basil, oregano, salt, pepper, and parsley (red pepper flakes, if using)
3. Dot with 1/2 of tomato paste.
4. Repeat layers.
5. Drizzle olive oil over top of final layer.
6. Cover and cook on low setting for 7-8 hours, until vegetable are tender.

# INDIAN VEGETABLE CURRY

Servings: 6

1 tablespoon coconut oil

1 small yellow onion, diced

3 clove garlic, minced

1 teaspoon cumin powder

½ teaspoon turmeric

½ teaspoon cardamom

½ teaspoon cinnamon

½ teaspoon ground ginger

1 medium sweet potato, peeled and cut into bit-size cubes

1 head cauliflower, cut into small florets

1 parsley root, diced

1 red pepper, diced

1 cup vegetable or chicken broth

1 can (15 ounces) coconut milk

Salt and freshly ground black pepper, to taste

Flat leaf parsley for garnish

1. Add all ingredients to slow cooker. Mix to combine.
2. Cover and cook on low setting for 4-5 hours until sweet potatoes are tender.
3. Serve hot, topped with fresh parsley for garnish.

# Seafood

# SEAFOOD STEW

Servings: 8

1 large onion, chopped

2 celery stalks, finely chopped

5 garlic cloves, minced

1 (28-ounce) can diced tomatoes, undrained

1 (8-ounce) bottle clam juice

1 (6-ounce) can tomato paste

1/2 cup water

1 tablespoon red wine vinegar

1 tablespoon olive oil

3 teaspoons Italian seasoning

1/4 teaspoon crushed red pepper flakes

1 bay leaf

1 pound firm-fleshed white fish, cut into 1-inch pieces (cod, haddock, tilapia)

3/4 pound medium shrimp, uncooked, tails removed

1 (6 1/2-ounce) can chopped clams with juice, undrained

1 (6-ounce) can crabmeat, drained

1/4 cup fresh parsley, chopped

1. In slow cooker, combine onions, celery, garlic, tomatoes, clam juice, tomato paste, wine, vinegar, oil, Italian seasoning, sugar, pepper flakes and bay leaf; mix well.
2. Cover and cook on high for 4 hours.
3. Add fish, shrimp, clams, and crabmeat. Cover, reduce heat to low, and cook for another 30 minutes to an hour, until fish flakes easily.
4. Remove bay leaf. Stir in parsley and serve.

# FISH CHOWDER

*This chowder is so rich and delicious, you won't even miss the cream.*

Servings: 6-8

3 pounds cod

2 pounds red potatoes, cubed (optional)

1 large sweet potato, peeled and cubed

1 onion, diced

2 large carrots, sliced

3 stalks celery

3 cloves garlic, minced

6 cups chicken broth

6 slices cooked bacon, crumbled

2 cans (10 ounce) coconut milk (not low-fat)

Sea salt and freshly ground black pepper, to taste

1. Add cod, potatoes, sweet potato, onion, carrots, celery, garlic, and chicken broth to slow cooker. Stir to combine.
2. Cover and cook on low for 6-8 hours.
3. Add cooked bacon, coconut milk, salt, and pepper. Stir, cover, and cook for an additional 30-45 minutes.
4. Serve and enjoy!

# THAI SPICY SOUP WITH SHRIMP, TOM YUM KUNG

*The combination of hot and sour flavors in this soup are very tasty.*

Servings: 6

6 cups shrimp stock (can substitute fish or vegetable stock)

1 inch piece fresh ginger, grated

3 stalks lemongrass, peeled and chopped (substitute: lemon zest)

1 cup shiitake mushrooms

1/4 cup fish sauce

3 tablespoons roasted red chili paste

1 pound shrimp, uncooked, peeled, deveined

Juice of 1 lime

1/2 cup cilantro, chopped

1/2 cup green onions

1. Place shrimp stock, ginger, lemongrass, mushrooms, fish sauce, and chili paste in slow cooker, mix well. Cover and cook on high setting for 2-3 hours.

2. Add shrimp, lime, and cilantro. Cover and cook on low setting for 40 to 45 minutes.

3. Serve garnished with green onion.

# Desserts

# SLOW COOKER BAKED APPLES

These smell like fresh-baked apple pie.

Servings: 6

6 large apples (any variety)

1/4 cup raisins

1/4 cup dried cranberries

1/4 cup honey

1 teaspoon cinnamon

3 tablespoons ghee

1. Core apples.
2. In a bowl, mix together the raisins, cranberries, honey and cinnamon. Divide mixture evenly and fill apples with 1/6 of mixture. Top with 1/2 tablespoon of ghee per apple.
3. Place apples in slow cooker. Add 1/2 inch of water to bottom.
4. Cook on low for 8-10 hours.

# PEAR CRUMBLE

*These are simply delicious!*

Servings: 6

6 pears, cut into quarters

1/4 cup maple syrup

1/2 cup water

1 teaspoon cinnamon

1 teaspoon ginger

1/2 teaspoon nutmeg

1. Put all ingredients into slow cooker.
2. Cover and cook on low setting for 4-5 hours.
3. Serve topped with a sprinkle of coconut sugar.

# PUMPKIN BREAD

*This pumpkin bread is not too sweet and very moist.*

Servings: 6

1/2 cup coconut oil

1/2 cup coconut sugar

2 eggs, beaten

1 (15 ounce) can pumpkin

1 1/2 cups coconut flour

1/2 teaspoon salt

1/2 teaspoon cinnamon

1/2 teaspoon nutmeg

1 teaspoon baking soda

1. In a large bowl, mix together the coconut oil and coconut sugar. Stir in eggs and pumpkin. Add dry ingredients and mix until well blended.
2. Pour batter into bread pan (grease with a little coconut oil or ghee). Place pan into slow cooker.
3. Cover and cook on high for 2 1/2 to 3 hours.

# BERRY COBBLER

Servings: 6

1 1/4 cups coconut flour, divided

1 cup plus 2 tablespoons coconut sugar, divided

1 teaspoon baking powder

1/2 teaspoon cinnamon

1 egg, beaten

1/4 cup coconut milk

2 tablespoons coconut oil

Pinch of sea salt

2 cups raspberries (thawed if frozen)

2 cups blueberries (thawed of frozen)

1. In a large bowl, combine 1 cup of flour, 2 tablespoons of sugar, baking powder, and cinnamon. Add in beaten egg, milk, and oil. Stir until just moistened.
2. Lightly grease bottom of slow cooker with a little coconut oil. Spread batter evenly into bottom of slow cooker.
3. In a bowl, combine remaining flow, sugar, salt, and berries. Toss gently to combine. Spread berries over batter evenly.
4. Cover and cook on high setting for about 2 1/2 hours or until toothpick inserted in center comes out clean.

# SLOW COOKER APPLESAUCE

*This slow cooker dish is definitely delicious.*

Servings: 6

10 apples, peeled and sliced

½ cup honey

¼ teaspoon cinnamon powder

¼ cup lemon juice

¼ teaspoon salt

¼ teaspoon ginger powder

1 ½ cups of water

1. Place all ingredients in slow cooker and stir to combine.
2. Cover and cook on low for 6 hours.
3. Apples should be very soft now and can be eaten as is. If you prefer smoother applesauce, place in blender or food processor and pulse until desired consistency is reached.
4. Serve warm or chill in refrigerator before serving.

# From the Author

I hope you enjoyed the *Paleo Slow Cooker Cookbook* and that it helps you create easy, healthy Paleo meals for you and your family to enjoy!

Please check out our other titles in the Paleo cooking series:

*Primal Paleo Cookbook: Quick and Easy Paleo Recipes*

*Paleo Diet: Beginner's Paleo Cooking for Health and Weight Loss*

*Mediterranean Paleo*

*Slow Cooker Paleo: Healthy, Quick, and Easy Paleo Recipes for Your Slow Cooker*

*Asian Paleo*

*Paleo Autoimmune Protocol: Paleo Recipes and Meal Plan to Heal Your Body*

# Index

## A

apples
   Hearty Turkey Stew with Root Vegetables and Apples 34
   Slow Cooker Applesauce 120
   Slow Cooker Baked Apples 116

## B

bacon
   Fish Chowder 111
   Meatball Soup 56
   Slow Cooker Bolognese Sauce 54
Barbecue Sauce 90, 92
beef
   Beef Bourguignon 74
   Beef Stew with Butternut Squash 49
   Ground Beef Sweet Potato Casserole 70
   Hungarian Beef Goulash 69
   Meatball Soup 56
   Moroccan Beef Tagine 62
   Oxtail Soup 77
   Paleo Beef Chili 50
   Paleo Italian Meatballs 52
   Peppers Stuffed with Spinach and Ground Beef 65
   Pot Roast with Root Vegetables 48
   Slow Cooker Beef Ragu with Zoodles 72
   Slow Cooker Beef Stew a la Catherine 71
   Slow Cooker Bolognese Sauce 54
   Slow Cooker Short Ribs 66
   Stuffed Cabbage Rolls 59
bell peppers
   Indian Vegetable Curry 106
   Peppers Stuffed with Spinach and Ground Beef 65
Berry Cobbler 119

## C

cabbage
   Stuffed Cabbage Rolls 59
carrots
   Beef Bourguignon 74
   Hearty Turkey Stew with Root Vegetables and Apples 34
   Irish Stew 80
   Pot Roast with Root Vegetables 48
   Slow Cooker Beef Stew a la Catherine 71
   Vegetarian Vegetable Stew 102
cauliflower
   Indian Vegetable Curry 106
   Slow Cooker Beef Stew a la Catherine 71
chicken
   Chicken and Shrimp Gumbo 40
   Chicken Cacciatore 42
   Chicken Curry 28
   Chicken Fajita Soup 36
   Chicken Gumbo 44
   Chicken Mole 25
   Chicken Tikka Masala 24
   Ginger-Orange Chicken 30
   Kimchi Chicken 41
   Mediterranean Savory Chicken Stew 31
   Moroccan Chicken Tagine 38
   Paleo Chicken Soup 22
   Slow Cooker Whole Chicken 37
   Teriyaki Wings 32
chili
   Paleo Beef Chili 50
clams
   Seafood Stew 110
crab
   Seafood Stew 110

## D

duck
   Slow-Cooked Roast Duck 27

## E

Eggplant Ragout/Ratatouille 104

## F

fish
   Fish Chowder 111
   Seafood Stew 110
freezer items 17

## G

gut health 13

## H

health benefits 13
healthy fats 13

## I

inflammation 13
Irish Stew 80

## K

Kale and Sausage Soup 88

## L

lamb
  Curry Braised Lamb Leg  82
  Irish Stew  80
  Lamb Shanks and Cremini Mushrooms  84
  Slow Cooker Lamb with Olives and Apricots  83
  Spicy Indian Lamb Curry  85

## M

meatballs
  Meatball Soup  56
  Paleo Italian Meatballs  52
minimum internal temperatures  19
mushrooms
  Beef Bourguignon  74
  Chicken Cacciatore  42
  Lamb Shanks and Cremini Mushrooms  84

## O

omega-3 fatty acids  13
omega-6 fatty acids  13
Oxtail Soup  77

## P

Paleo diet
  about  12
  health benefits of  13
Paleo ingredients  15–17
pantry items  15–17
parsnip
  Irish Stew  80
Pear Crumble  117
polyunsaturated fatty acids (PUFAs)  13
pork
  Herbed Pork Roast  91
  Kale and Sausage Soup  88
  Kalua Pork  97
  Meatball Soup  56
  Paleo Beef Chili  50
  Paleo Italian Meatballs  52
  Pepper Pork Chops with Dried Apricots  94
  Pork Chili Verde  95
  Pork Spareribs with Homemade Barbecue Sauce  90
  Pulled Pork with Barbecue Sauce  92
  Slow-Cooked Pork Carnitas  96
  Stuffed Cabbage Rolls  59
Pumpkin Bread  118

## R

refrigerator items  17
ribs
  Pork Spareribs with Homemade Barbecue Sauce  90
  Slow Cooker Short Ribs  66
rutabaga
  Pot Roast with Root Vegetables  48

## S

sausage
  Kale and Sausage Soup  88
seafood
  Chicken and Shrimp Gumbo  40
  Fish Chowder  111
  Seafood Stew  110
  Thai Spicy Soup with Shrimp  112
shrimp
  Chicken and Shrimp Gumbo  40
  Seafood Stew  110
  Thai Spicy Soup with Shrimp  112
slow cookers
  about  18–19
  choosing  18
  tips for using  18
soups and stews
  Beef Stew with Butternut Squash  49
  Chicken Fajita Soup  36
  Fish Chowder  111
  Hungarian Beef Goulash  69
  Irish Stew  80
  Kale and Sausage Soup  88
  Meatball Soup  56
  Mediterranean Savory Chicken Stew  31
  Oxtail Soup  77
  Paleo Chicken Soup  22
  Seafood Stew  110
  Slow Cooker Beef Stew a la Catherine  71
  Thai Spicy Soup with Shrimp  112
  Vegetarian Vegetable Stew  102
sour cream  69
spinach
  Peppers Stuffed with Spinach and Ground Beef  65
squash
  Beef Stew with Butternut Squash  49
  Eggplant Ragout/Ratatouille  104
  Slow Cooker Beef Stew a la Catherine  71
  Vegetarian Vegetable Stew  102
standard American diet (SAD)  13
sweet potatoes
  Fish Chowder  111
  Ground Beef Sweet Potato Casserole  70
  Hearty Turkey Stew with Root Vegetables and Apples  34
  Indian Vegetable Curry  106
  Sweet Potato Coconut Curry  100

## T

turkey
  Chicken Gumbo  44
  Hearty Turkey Stew with Root Vegetables and Apples  34

turnips
  Pot Roast with Root Vegetables  48
  Vegetarian Vegetable Stew  102

## V

Veal Osso Busco  60
Vegetarian Vegetable Stew  102

## W

weight loss  13

## Z

Zoodles  72

zucchini
  Slow Cooker Beef Ragu with Zoodles  72
  Vegetarian Vegetable Stew  102

# More Bestselling Titles from Dylanna Press

*Mason Jar Meals* by Dylanna Press

Mason jar meals are a fun and practical way to take your meals on the go. Mason jars are an easy way to prepare individual servings, so whether you're cooking for one, two, or a whole crowd, these fun, make-ahead meals will work.

**Includes More than 50 Recipes and Full-Color Photos**

In this book, you'll find a wide variety of recipes including all kinds of salads, as well as hot meal ideas such as mini chicken pot pies and lasagna in a jar. Also included are mouth-watering desserts such as strawberry shortcake, apple pie, and s'mores.

The recipes are easy to prepare and don't require any special cooking skills. So what are you waiting for? Grab your Mason jars and start preparing these gorgeous and tasty dishes!

*The Inflammation Diet* by Dylanna Press

**Beat Pain, Slow Aging, and Reduce Risk of Heart Disease with the Inflammation Diet**

Inflammation has been called the "silent killer" and it has been linked to a wide variety of illnesses including heart disease, arthritis, diabetes, chronic pain, autoimmune disorders, and cancer.

Often, the root of chronic inflammation is in the foods we eat.

**The Inflammation Diet: Complete Guide to Beating Pain and Inflammation** will show you how, by making simple changes to your diet, you can greatly reduce inflammation in your body and reduce your symptoms and lower your risk of chronic disease.

**The book includes a complete plan for eliminating inflammation and implementing an anti-inflammatory diet:**

• Overview of inflammation and the body's immune response – what can trigger it and why chronic inflammation is harmful
• The link between diet and inflammation
• Inflammatory foods to avoid
• Anti-inflammatory foods to add to your diet to beat pain and inflammation
• Over 50 delicious inflammation diet recipes
• A 14-day meal plan

Take charge of your health and implement the inflammation diet to lose weight, slow the aging process, eliminate chronic pain, and reduce the likelihood and symptoms of chronic disease.

Learn how to heal your body from within through diet.

www.ingramcontent.com/pod-product-compliance
Lightning Source LLC
Chambersburg PA
CBHW081336080526
44588CB00017B/2640